FLIGHT
HELICOPTERS

June Loves

This edition first published in 2002 in the United States of America by Chelsea House
Publishers, a subsidiary of Haights Cross Communications

Chelsea House Publishers
1974 Sproul Road, Suite 400
Broomall, PA 19008-0914

The Chelsea House world wide web address is www.chelseahouse.com

Library of Congress Cataloging-in-Publication Data Applied for.
ISBN 0-7910-6562-6

First published in 2000 by
Macmillan Education Australia Pty Ltd
627 Chapel Street, South Yarra, Australia, 3141

Text copyright © June Loves 2000

Edited by Lara Whitehead
Text design by if Design
Cover design by if Design
Page layout by if Design/Raul Diche
Illustrations by Lorenzo Lucia
Printed in Hong Kong

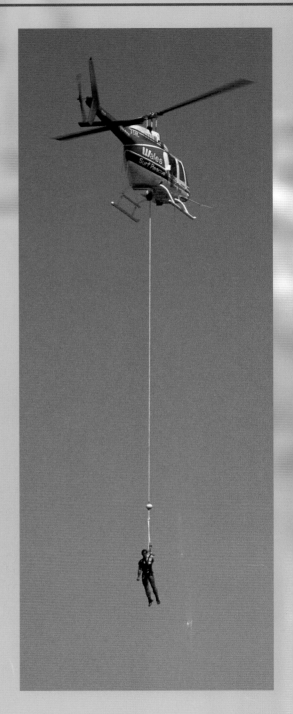

Acknowledgements
The author and the publisher are grateful to the following for permission to reproduce
copyright material:

Cover: helicopter (center) and Wales rescue helicopter (background), courtesy of
Coo-ee Picture Library.

Photographs courtesy of: Australian Picture Library/Roy Bisson, pp. 10–1; Australian Picture
Library/Corbis-Bettmann, pp. 4, 8–9; Australian War Memorial, p. 9; Coo-ee Historical Picture
Library, p. 6; Coo-ee Picture Library, pp. 2, 3, 12–3, 15, 20–1, 24, 25, 26, 27, 28–9, 30–1, 32;
Great Southern Stock, pp. 16-7, 18–9, 22, 23, 28 (top right); Lochman Transparencies/Brian
Downs, p. 7; Mary Evans Picture Library, p. 5 (bottom).

While every care has been taken to trace and acknowledge copyright the publishers
tender their apologies for any accidental infringement where copyright has proved
untraceable.

Contents

Early helicopters

THE FIRST HELICOPTER DESIGNS

Leonardo da Vinci was a famous Italian artist, sculptor, scientist and engineer who lived in the fifteenth century. In his drawings were designs for a helicopter and other remarkable flying devices.

Leonardo da Vinci is believed to be the first person to use scientific experiments to investigate flight. His helicopter design had a spiral wing, like an airscrew. The helicopter was designed to be able to screw itself up into the air. His designs were only discovered late in the nineteenth century and by this time the helicopter had been reinvented.

Leonardo da Vinci's drawing of a helicopter with two revolving propellers.

FLYING ON ROTATING WINGS

The idea of flying on rotating wings, like the **hovering** flight of the hummingbird and the bee, fascinated many pioneer aviation inventors. However, the helicopter was one of the most difficult flight machines to perfect. It proved very difficult to design and build a helicopter that was stable and controllable in the air.

THE FIRST HELICOPTER FLIGHT

There were many attempts at building 'hovering' machines. The first helicopter to lift from the ground was the Breguet-Richet Gyroplane No. 1 in September 1907. However, it proved to be unstable and had to be steadied by four people using long poles.

THE SECOND HELICOPTER FLIGHT

The French inventor Paul Cornu designed and built the first full-scale helicopter capable of lifting a person off the ground. He called his machine the 'Flying Breeze'. Although Paul Cornu's helicopter only lifted off the ground for 20 seconds, to a height of about 30 centimeters (11.8 inches), it is recognized as the first manned helicopter to make a free flight. This was in November, 1907.

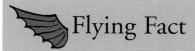

Flying Fact

The word 'helicopter' comes from the Greek *helix* (a screw) and *pteron* (a wing).

Helicopters are known as 'rotary-wing' aircraft. Their controls are different from ordinary fixed-wing airplanes.

Paul Cornu in his helicopter, 1907.

The autogyro

THE BREAKTHROUGH in building a successful helicopter came with the invention of a plane without wings, the **autogyro**.

The autogyro was first built by Juan de la Cierva. It had a normal engine and fuselage like an airplane but used a spinning wing, or **rotor**, mounted above the **fuselage** instead of fixed wings. The rotor provided lift for short take-offs but the autogyro could not move sideways or hover like a helicopter..

The autogyro had limited success. It could not hover or take off straight up into the air but it encouraged the development of the true helicopter. It also showed how flapping hinges for rotor blades could be successful.

A SNAIL'S PACE

The Cierva C-20 was flown very slowly into the wind. It could be outpaced by a person running!

Rotor blades with hinges to provide lift

G-ACIN

Fabric-covered tube and steel fuselage similar to a biplane

Hanging control column to allow the pilot to tilt the blades in any direction

Propeller to pull the autogryro forward for take-off and normal flight

An autogyro flying over London in 1935.

CREATING LIFT WITHOUT ENGINES

The most important difference between the autogryro and the helicopter is that the rotor of the autogyro is not driven by the engine, as in a helicopter. The autogyro's rotors turn because of air pressure as the aircraft is pulled forward by its propeller.

MODERN AUTOGYROS

Modern autogyros are often flown for fun. An autogyro takes off by moving along the ground, just like an airplane. The rotor then turns and provides the lift for take-off. The engine drives the propeller, not the rotor as in true helicopters.

A modern autogyro.

EARLY MOTORCAR?

In the 1930s, many people believed that autogyros would be like motor cars. Companies who made autogyros suggested that people could hop into one at their house, fly into the air and avoid traffic jams.

The first helicopter

THE FIRST HELICOPTERS to take off and stay in the air for a reasonable time were built in the 1930s but it was 1939 before the problems of helicopters were solved.

Before this time, helicopters could lift off the ground but they were unstable and often flipped over. The German Henrich Focke built a machine with two main rotors. In 1937, it flew for more than one hour. It was between 1939 and 1942 that Igor Sikorsky designed and built the first successful helicopter. The Sikorsky VS-300 was a single-seater helicopter with a main rotor and a **tail rotor**. It was the first true helicopter as we know them today.

Igor Sikorsky making the first successful controlled helicopter flight, 1940.

IGOR SIKORSKY

When he was a child, Igor Sikorsky was fascinated by the thought of rotor-winged flight. As a teenager he conducted many experiments with helicopters. When he migrated to the United States from Russia in 1917, he was already a well-known airplane designer. In the 1930s, Sikorsky worked on his designs for a powered helicopter. In 1939, he developed the VS-300. He pioneered the helicopter design that has been used ever since.

THE R-4

Igor Sikorsky improved his VS-300 design and called it the R-4. The US Army placed a large order for the R-4 in 1942. There were more than 400 helicopters built by the end of World War II in 1945.

A Sikorsky R-4 taking off, 1945.

DID YOU KNOW?

'Chopper' and 'bird' are slang terms for a helicopter.

Parts of a helicopter

A HELICOPTER IS the most versatile of all aircraft. It can fly forward backward and sideways. It can lift into the air from a standing position and also hover in the sky. A helicopter can land on a small space and on most surfaces.

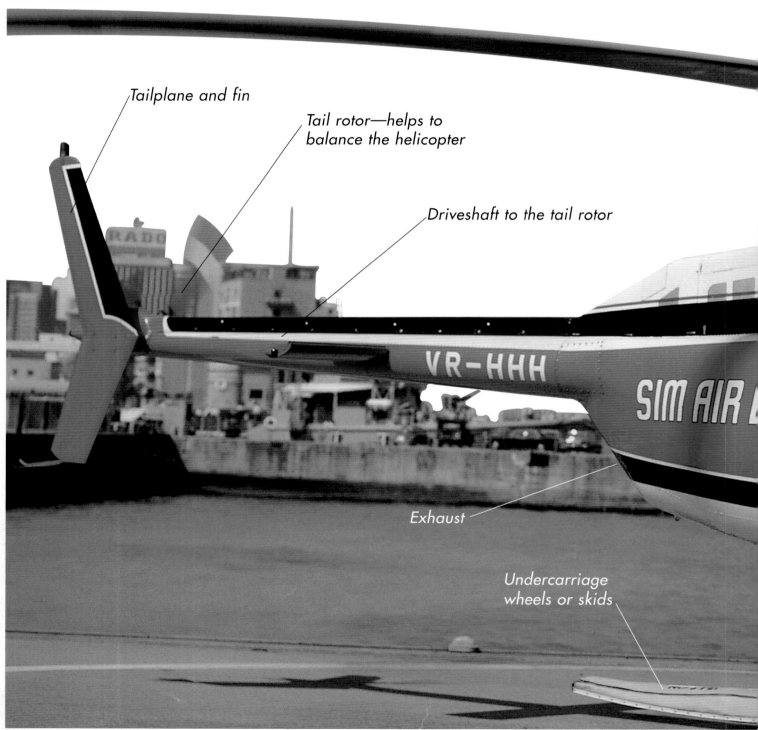

Tailplane and fin

Tail rotor—helps to balance the helicopter

Driveshaft to the tail rotor

Exhaust

Undercarriage wheels or skids

VR-HHH

SIM AIR

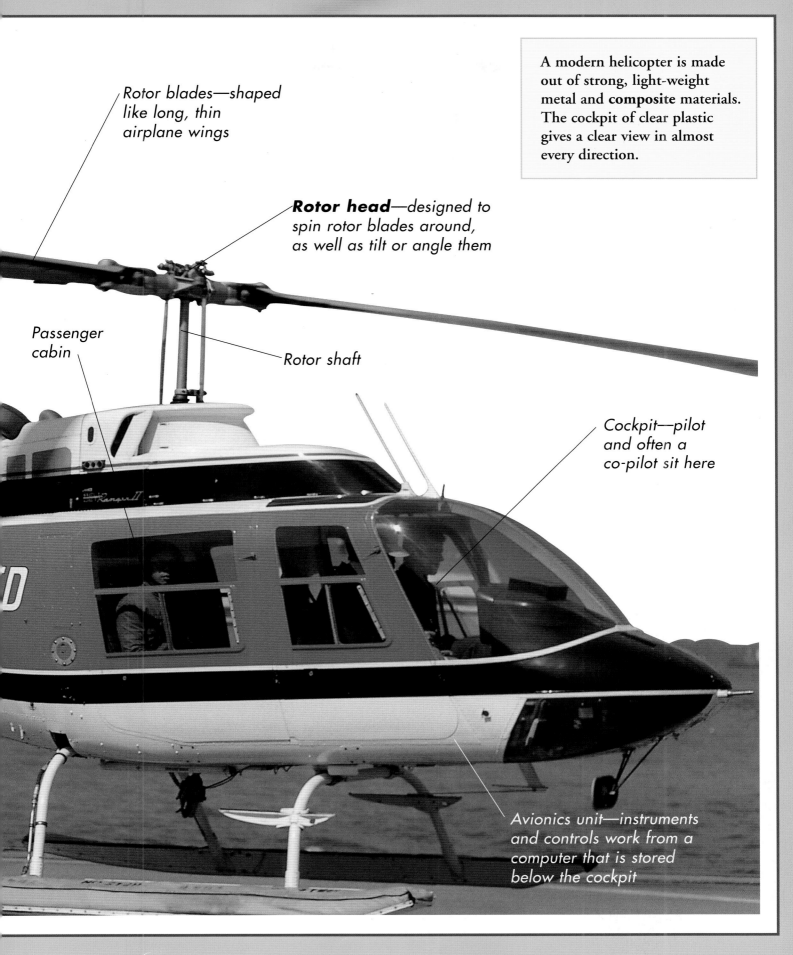

Rotor blades—shaped like long, thin airplane wings

Rotor head—designed to spin rotor blades around, as well as tilt or angle them

Rotor shaft

Passenger cabin

A modern helicopter is made out of strong, light-weight metal and **composite** materials. The cockpit of clear plastic gives a clear view in almost every direction.

Cockpit—pilot and often a co-pilot sit here

Avionics unit—instruments and controls work from a computer that is stored below the cockpit

How helicopters fly

HELICOPTERS AND AIRPLANES look very different, yet they both use the air to fly. An airplane has to move forward very quickly in order to fly. This allows the air to rapidly pass under and over its wings and produce **lift**.

A helicopter's engine whirls its rotor around so that the blades cut through the air to produce enough lift to fly. Because the helicopter does not have to move forward to do this, it can rise straight up into the sky.

The rotor of a helicopter forces air down to raise the helicopter off the ground. The rotor not only provides lift but when tilted slightly it provides **propulsion**, or **thrust**, in the desired direction.

THE MAIN ROTOR

The blades of a helicopter are called the rotors. A helicopter's blades work together like an overhead propeller, lifting the helicopter through the air. The rotor blades have an airfoil shape, more curved above than below. Changing the angle of the rotor blades (the **pitch**) changes the amount of lifting force they produce. When the whole rotor assembly is tilted in any direction, part of the lifting force moves the helicopter in that direction—forwards, backwards or sideways.

Most helicopters have one main rotor in the front and a smaller rotor on the tail. Some large helicopters, called **tandems**, have two main rotors, one at the front and one at the back.

TAIL ROTOR

The tail rotor provides the sideways force to stop the helicopter from spinning in the opposite direction to the way the main rotor is spinning. This is known as the torque effect. The tail rotor is also used as a rudder for steering. The pilot changes the angle on its blades to swing the tail left or right.

THE ROTOR HEAD

The most important working part of a helicopter is the rotor head. It is the piece of machinery in the center of the rotor blades. The rotor head is made up of many different parts that help to turn or angle the blades to change the direction of the helicopter.

The movable control rods in the rotor head alter the angle or pitch of each rotor blade as well as the tilt of the whole rotor unit. The rotor head is driven by the helicopter's engines.

MOVING FORWARD, BACKWARD AND SIDEWAYS

Helicopters can fly in all directions as well as hover in one spot. They can do this because they get both lift and thrust from the spinning rotor.

The main rotor moves the helicopter forward, backward or sideways through the air. The rotor provides the vertical lifting force to keep the helicopter in the air but the pilot can also control the whole rotor so that it tips forward, backward or sideways. The lift force then has a component that acts to move the helicopter in the required direction as well as simply keeping it in the air.

Making the lift equal to its weight causes the helicopter to hover.

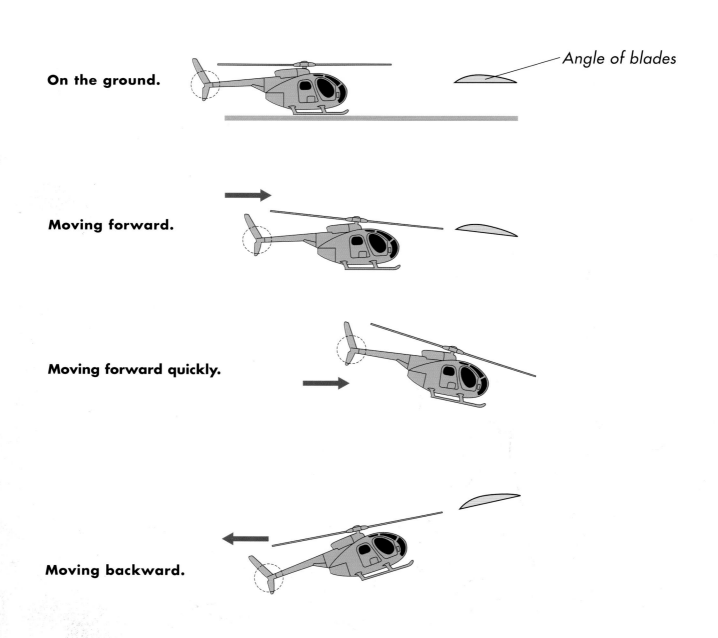

On the ground.

Angle of blades

Moving forward.

Moving forward quickly.

Moving backward.

Rescue helicopters can winch people
to safety while they hover above.

Flying a helicopter

ALTHOUGH ITS INSTRUMENTS are like those of an airplane, a helicopter is more complicated to fly because it can hover and move in all directions. The helicopter pilot must handle several controls at once. Some helicopters have two sets of controls, one for the pilot and one for the co-pilot. Many helicopters have computer-controlled automatic pilot systems.

Inside the cockpit, there are three main controls that the pilot uses: the collective pitch control, the control columns and the rudder pedals.

COLLECTIVE PITCH CONTROL

The collective pitch control is used to control the pitch (angle) of the rotor blades and the power delivered to the blades by the engine. It has a twist-grip for controlling engine power. Pulling up the collective pitch control provides increased lift. Using the collective pitch control to change the pitch of the rotor blades varies the amount of lift. The greater the pitch, the greater the lift. Lowering the collective pitch control reduces lift so that the helicopter hovers or descends.

The cockpit controls of a helicopter.

CONTROL COLUMNS

Pilots use the control columns to produce forward, backward or sideways flight. The control lever is like the joystick in an airplane. It is used for banking or turning the helicopter, as well as climbing or descending. It tilts the main rotor unit forward, backward or sideways to direct the helicopter's flight. Tilting the rotor unit forward makes the helicopter fly forward.

RUDDER PEDALS

Pilot uses their feet to operate the rudder pedals. The pedals work the tail rotor, which controls the direction in which the helicopter points. They change the pitch (angle) of the tail rotor blades.

Helicopter engines

THE HELICOPTERS BUILT in the 1930s and 1940s were powered by gasoline engines, similar to car engines. In the 1950s, a new type of jet engine called a **turboshaft** was developed. It produced more power and used kerosene, a less expensive and less flammable fuel than gasoline.

Today, modern helicopters still use turboshaft engines. Many helicopters are fitted with two engines. Two engines can provide more power than a single engine. In the event of one engine failing, the remaining engine enables the pilot to make a safe, controlled landing.

With the invention of the turboshaft engine, fast all-purpose helicopters were designed and built in the 1950s and 1960s. Jetranger is a small, fast, all-purpose helicopter that can carry up to five people at speeds of 210 kilometers (130.5 miles) per hour. It is used for a wide range of tasks.

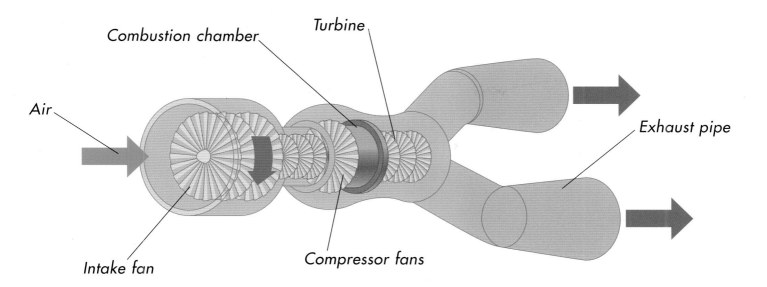

Air

Combustion chamber

Turbine

Exhaust pipe

Intake fan

Compressor fans

A turboshaft engine.

TURBOSHAFT ENGINES

A turboshaft engine is a type of jet engine. It turns a **shaft** rather than giving off a stream of hot gases as gasoline-driven combustion engines do. The turning shaft drives the main rotor and the tail rotor through sets of gears.

How a turboshaft engine works

- Air is sucked into the front of the engine by an intake fan.

- The air flows through compressor fans that guide it into the **combustion chamber**.

- In the combustion chamber, fuel is sprayed into the pressurized air and ignited.

- The burning mixture of fuel and air heats up, expands and is forced through the engine to the exhaust pipe.

- On the way to the exhaust, the hot gases pass through a **turbine** and make it turn.

- The turbine provides the power to turn the helicopter's rotor shaft through a gear box.

Taking off and landing

TAKING OFF

Before a helicopter can take off, the engines must make the rotor blades spin fast enough to provide the necessary lift.

When the pilot pulls up the collective pitch control, the angle of the rotor blades is increased. Air flowing over the top of the blade travels faster than the air underneath. This reduces air pressure above the blade and creates lift.

With the right combination of rotor speed and blade angle, enough lift is produced for the helicopter to take off. Helicopters usually take off pointing into the wind because the wind provides extra lift.

When the pilot starts the motor, the rotor blades spin around but the helicopter stays on the ground.

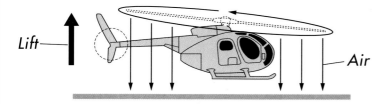

Lift   Air

When the pilot uses the controls to increase the angle of the rotor blades and to operate the rotor at a fast rotor speed, more lift is produced. The air is forced down and the helicopter begins to rise.

The seeds of the sycamore, maple and ash trees are shaped like rotor blades. When the seeds fall from the tree, they gently spin and are carried to a new place to grow.

LANDING

Helicopters rarely land vertically because a pilot cannot see directly underneath the helicopter. The pilot also cannot be sure its tail will not be knocked by some object. Another problem is that the downdraft from the rotor blades disturbs the airflow underneath the helicopter. This causes **turbulence** that can rock the helicopter.

To avoid these problems, helicopters are usually brought in to land at an angle, called a glide-slope.

To make the helicopter lose height, the pilot reduces engine power and lowers the collective pitch control to decrease the angle of the rotor blades.

Flying Fact

To take off, an ordinary fixed-wing airplane has to gain speed along the ground. It can take off only when it is going fast enough for the wings to produce enough lift.

Emergency landing

If a helicopter's engines fail, the air that rushes through its rotor blades as it descends makes them spin. This allows the helicopter to descend safely if the rotor speed is kept high by decreasing the rotor blade angle until the helicopter is just above the ground. Here the angle is increased suddenly to provide enough lift to stop the descent and allow the helicopter to land gently. This maneuver requires fine judgment by the pilot.

Landing gear

As helicopters can land on most surfaces including water and snow, they have different types of undercarriages for the particular landing surfaces.

Some helicopters, such as the AS 355 Twinstar, have **skids** instead of wheels as an undercarriage to stop them rolling when landing on uneven ground.

Navigating in a helicopter

IN CLEAR WEATHER, helicopter pilots can navigate visually using maps. Helicopters can also have the same modern electronic navigation aids as fixed-wing aircraft. These allow the pilot to navigate when they are not able to see clearly. Radar systems in modern helicopters help to navigate at night or in bad weather conditions, such as when it is hazy, foggy, cloudy or raining.

PENCIL-AND-MAP METHOD OF NAVIGATION

Helicopter pilots are still trained to use and understand the basic pencil-and-map method of navigation like the early airplane pilots. The pilots fly a steady course on the compass and hold a steady airspeed. They use their maps to constantly identify landmarks below so that they know exactly where they are. By using an accurate watch or **chronometer**, the pilots can measure their ground speed and work out how long it should take to travel to a particular place.

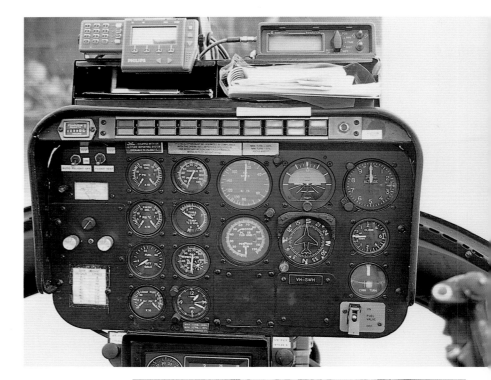

FLIGHT PLAN

Before taking off, the helicopter pilot may have to file a flight plan. The flight plan shows the helicopter's route, time it should take to reach its destination, and the height and speed at which it will fly.

Air traffic controllers use radar screens to track aircraft in flight.

WEATHER RADAR

Many modern helicopters have weather radar equipment in their nose cones to locate bad weather ahead. The radar beams reflect off water droplets in clouds up to 300 kilometers (186 miles) ahead, showing where bad weather lies. This information is displayed on a screen in the helicopter's instrument panel.

How radar works

'Radar' is short for radio detection and ranging. Radar works by sending out short bursts of radio signals. The radio signals bounce off any object they hit, like echoes. The radar's computer works out how far away the object is based on the time the signals take to bounce back. Radio signals would take 1/500th of a second to return from an object 300 kilometers (186 miles) away, for example.

Types of helicopters

HELICOPTERS ARE DESIGNED and built in many different shapes and sizes depending on the tasks they are going to be used for and the conditions they will fly in. Helicopters can carry cargo, people, weapons or a mixture of these.

A helicopter uses a large amount of fuel because the engine provides all of the lifting force. Helicopters are expensive to maintain so they are used mainly for specialist tasks such as search and rescue, business transport and military use where the cost is justified.

PASSENGER HELICOPTERS

Lightweight passenger helicopters may carry as few as two people, including the pilot. They are often used to carry commuters to work in busy cities or to transport business people to nearby cities. Many city buildings have **helipads** so helicopters can land on their roofs.

The Boeing Vertol 234 is one of the largest passenger helicopters. It can carry up to 44 people. It has main rotors at the back and front called tandem rotors. These helicopters are called Chinooks when used by military forces.

A Boeing Vertol 234, also known as a Chinook.

This helicopter is riding on a helipad boat.

Sightseeing

Passenger helicopters are often used for sight-seeing flights. They can take tourists close to spectacular scenery and hover while the passengers enjoy the view.

HELIPADS

Helicopters can land on a very small area. Many city buildings and offshore oil rigs have a special landing pad called a helipad for helicopters. Helicopters are used for carrying workers and supplies to oil rigs. It is usually safer to travel by air than in a boat through rough seas.

HEAVY-LIFT HELICOPTERS

Heavy-lift helicopters usually have twin rotors and are used to lift and carry heavy loads. Goods and equipment may be carried inside or slung from a wire under the body. A large helicopter such as a Bell 205A-1 can lift as much as two metric tons (2.2 tons), the weight of two average cars.

Special helicopters are used as cranes to lift heavy machinery and equipment such as bulldozers. Some helicopters can lift sections of bridges, small houses, cars and even add extra structures such as spires to the tops of buildings. Special crane helicopters can lift ten metric tons (11 tons) or more.

FIRE FIGHTING

Helicopters play a very important part in fire fighting. They can dump and spray water on forest fires in remote areas. Helicopters used for fire fighting are specially fitted with tanks and equipment.

COMMUNITY REPORTING

Radio and television stations assist their audience by reporting on the traffic in and around large cities from helicopters. Some helicopters are used as shark patrols over popular beaches. They report back on sightings of sharks for swimmers and surfers.

A heavy-lift helicopter has extra-long rotor blades to increase its lifting ability.

POLICE HELICOPTERS

Police helicopters are used for monitoring road traffic. They can spot problems such as speeding and accidents. Police helicopters are also used to follow criminal suspects, as well as in search and rescue work.

AGRICULTURAL HELICOPTERS

Helicopters are used to assist farmers in many tasks such as spraying crops with fertilizers to help crops grow or insecticides to kill pests. Helicopters are also used in herding cattle and other animals on big properties.

SEARCH AND RESCUE HELICOPTERS

A helicopter's ability to take off and land straight up and down, and to hover motionless in the air, makes it suitable for rescue work. They are frequently used in rescue operations and assist in saving lives every year. Rescue helicopters can reach climbers stranded on mountains or people cut off by forest fires. Helicopters are often used to rescue people from sinking ships at sea.

Search and rescue helicopters have a winch and a cable that runs over a pulley above the main cabin door. The winches are operated by a powerful electric motor. Rescue crews use the winches to hoist people to safety.

In some helicopters the cabin can be changed for use as an ambulance. After a rescue, medical staff can treat injured survivors in the cabin while they fly to hospital.

MILITARY HELICOPTERS

The helicopter's ability to reach inaccessible places is important in times of war and peace. All-round helicopters are used for search and rescue work by armies, navies and air forces. They are also used for carrying troops and evacuations.

Armed helicopters fitted with weapon systems can be used to attack targets such as enemy tanks, ships or submarines.

Anti-submarine helicopters

Some military helicopters carry equipment and radar to track down submarines. These helicopters are ship-based and can take off and land from helipads or flight decks on the ships. Anti-submarine helicopters can carry torpedoes and missiles to destroy submarines.

Sonobuoys are microphones that are dropped into the water to pick up underwater noises, including the sounds of ships and submarine engines.

Dunking sonar is used to send out powerful sound waves. It is lowered on a line into the sea where it sends out sound waves. They are bounced back as echoes from big or hard objects and are heard through headphones worn by the operator in the helicopter.

Military helicopters are often used to transport troops to remote areas.

Flight timeline

1783 In France the brothers Joseph and Etienne Montgolfier launch the first successful hot-air balloon.

1852 The first steam-powered airship is flown by the French engineer Henri Giffard.

1890s The German engineer Otto Lilenthal builds and flies monoplane and biplane gliders.

1903 The Wright brothers make the first powered-aircraft flight at Kitty Hawk, the United States.

1909 French pilot Louis Bleriot makes the first successful airplane flight across the English Channel.

1910 The first commercial air service is established by Count Ferdinand von Zeppelin of Germany, using airships.

1914 World War I begins. Aircraft are used on both sides.

1919 Two British pilots, John Alcock and Arthur Whitten Brown, make the first non-stop flight across the Atlantic.

1927 The US pilot Charles Lindberg flies his Spirit of St. Louis solo across the Atlantic from New York to Paris.

1930 Frank Whittle of Great Britain takes out a patent for a jet engine.

1939 The first jet aircraft, the German He178, makes its first flight.

World War II begins. Aircraft are used on both sides.

American engineer Igor Sikorsky designs the first modern helicopter.

1947 Charles 'Chuck' Yeager breaks the sound barrier in the American Bell X-1 rocket plane, the first supersonic aircraft.

1952 The world's first jet airliner, the DeHavilland Comet, enters regular passenger service in the UK.

1970 The Boeing 747 jumbo jet enters service.

1975 The supersonic Concorde, the world's fastest airliner, goes into transatlantic service.

1984 The X-29, the experimental plane, flies for the first time.

1986 Dick Rutan and Jeana Yeager make the first unrefuelled round-the-world flight in the Rutan Voyager.

1989 The B-2 Stealth bomber is test flown.

1999 Bernard Piccard and Brian Jones, a Swiss doctor and a British pilot, fly around the world in a hot-air balloon.

2000 and beyond New supersonic space planes may be flying around the world carrying passengers and cargo in record-breaking times. Airships may provide regular passenger and cargo services. The International Space Station (ISS) will be fully functional by 2004. Astronauts and scientists will commute between Earth and the ISS to live and work in space. People may be flying between Earth and outer space as they live and work in bases on the moon and other planets.

Glossary

autogyro	an aircraft that uses a propeller for thrust and an unpowered rotor for lift
chronometer	an instrument used to measure time
combustion chamber	the part of an engine where the fuel is mixed with air and burned
composite	a material made up of several different materials
fuselage	the body of an aircraft
helipad	a special landing and take-off station for helicopters. A landing area with facilities such as fuel pumps or workshops is called a heliport
hover	to hang in the air without moving in any direction
lift	the force that raises an aircraft off the ground and keeps it in the air. In helicopters, the lift is provided by the rotor blades
pitch	the angle of the rotor blade
propulsion	something that pushes forward
rotor head	machinery designed to spin rotor blades around, as well as tilt or angle them
rotor	spinning wings of a helicopter or autogyro. In helicopters, rotors are driven by the engine. A rotor has two to eight blades
shaft	a central bar on which a turbine is fixed
skids	undercarriage gear that looks like tubes. It is used for landing on rough ground
tail rotor	small rotor blades on the tail that help to balance the helicopter
tandem rotors	two main rotors—one at the front and one at the back of a helicopter
thrust	a force that pushes forward
turbine	a set of fan-shaped blades on a shaft that spin when air or water moves through them
turboshaft	a type of jet engine that produces more power than a gasoline engine and uses kerosene for fuel
turbulence	violent movement of the air

Index